I0441984

Floral Coloring Book

Floral Coloring Book for Adults containing Roses, lilies, Floral Patterns and Flowers.

by Amanda Davenport

ISBN-13: 978-1522898801

ISBN-10: 1522898808

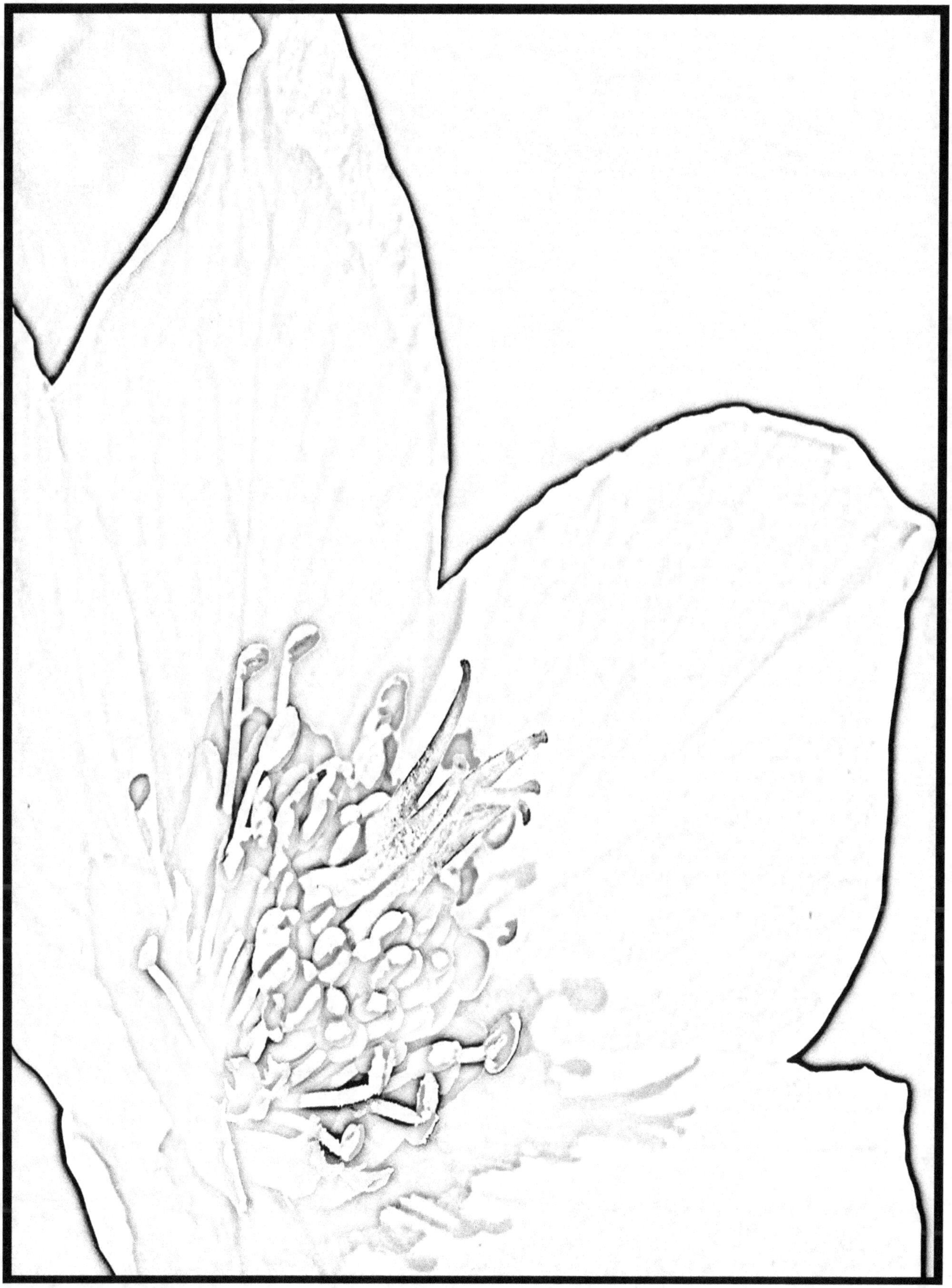

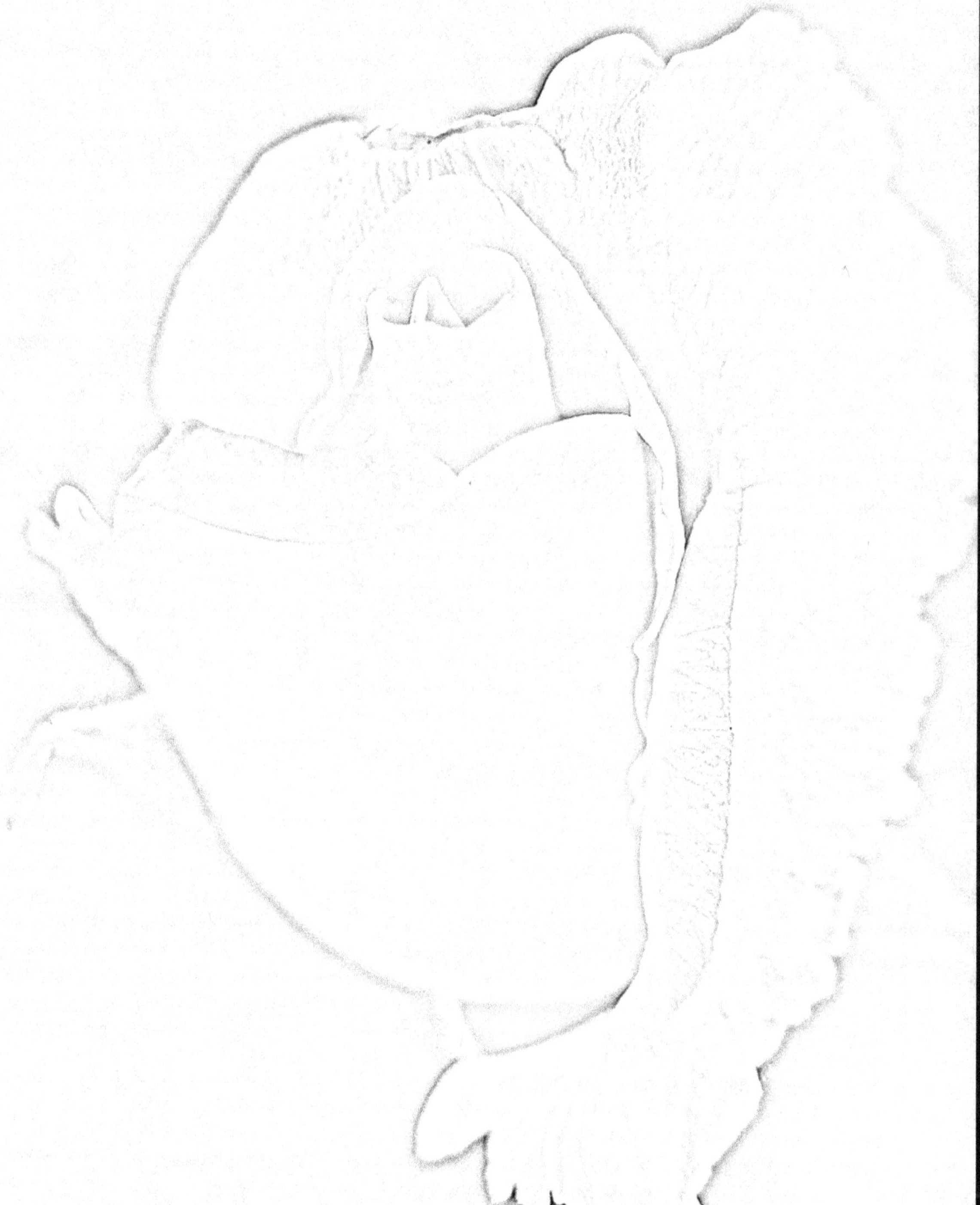

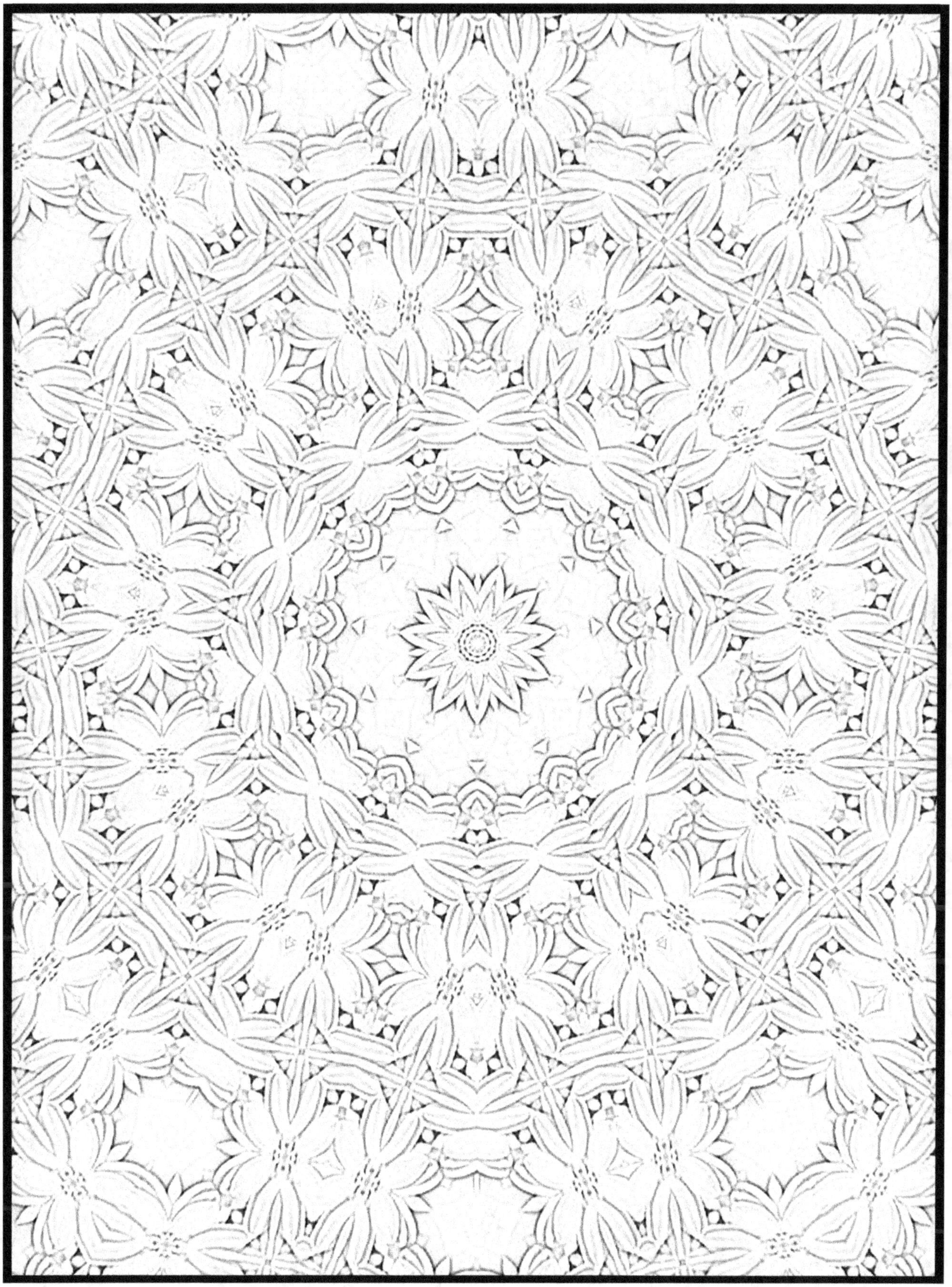

www.ingramcontent.com/pod-product-compliance
Lightning Source LLC
Chambersburg PA
CBHW081423280526
45788CB00009B/3214
9781522898801